The Wanderer's Waves

About the author

Tade Aina, a Nigerian, Pan-Africanist, scholar, activist, sociologist and Foundation Executive, has worked and published extensively on urbanization, higher education, development, social movements and philanthropy. He has published in literary magazines and edited collections. *The Wanderer's Waves* is his first full collection of poems. Tade has lived in Cairo, Dakar, Lagos, London, Nairobi, New York and Sussex.

The Wanderer's Waves

Poems

Tade Aina

Published by Amalion 2022

Amalion
BP 5637 Dakar-Fann
Dakar CP 10700
Senegal
http://www.amalion.net

ISBN 978-2-35926-111-0 Paperback
ISBN 978-2-35926-112-7 Ebook

© Tade Akin Aina

Poems in this collection previously published are "Dakar", "Kampala", "Merry Me Tonight", "Deadline", "A Cock Crows Outside My Window", "Stirrings at Dawn" and an earlier version of "Mouths Are Made for Better Things..." in *Maple Tree Literary Supplement*, Issue 24, 2019. "How Do We Sing a Song to Fifty Years in Dependence?" first published in *Poems for a Century: An Anthology on Nigeria*, Edited by Tope Omoniyi, Amalion Publishing, 2014.

Author photograph © Tade Akin Aina

Cover designed by Anke Rosenlöcher

For Mama Yaba,
Claudiana Atinuke Aina (née Reis), 1924–2016.

Contents

Lagos and New York

Entrances

To David Diop and Christopher Okigbo

Your voices,
cries and verses heard
at the dawn of my first journey.
You, the lonely Voice of Africa,
strumming the Kora in the hearts of whiteness.
You, the prodigal Celebrant
at Heavensgate's altar of Mother Idoto.
My inspiration across many lives,
wandering slippery straits to Cavafy's elusive Ithaca
in encounters with peoples, times and places,
demons and deities defied and deified.
Strange ports and tales told in different tongues,
to your shores I return, bearing stories and songs.

Drums

I sat taut,
my body, rhythms of tension,
waiting. How long does one
wait in this passing world
for the flash that is the answer
to the streams that daily drench the body?

"When will the answer come?,"
shouts the seeker's frustrated self
at confusion's crossroads. Crablike,
I pick my ways in sideways motion,
all senses, a torch in this maze,
as the reply throbs through my haze.

Drums of pain deafen my ears,
drums of joy my heart beats,
drums… drums… drums…
drums of what drum what?

Drums that change,
that the deaf picks,
the mute hums,
the blind sees,
the lame wins,
and the poor and the burdened all unite
to unhinge our painful yoke.

Drums of pain deafen my ears,
drums of joy beat my heart,
drums… drums… drums…
drums of what drum what?

Times

The times created me
in silk cloud tufts
that weave sun-lit robes.

The times created me
in tiny gold spores
floating and shimmering in the wind.

The times created me
in joyful pangs
music to Nature midwife's ears.

And I create the times
in silver reels
threaded across borders
unending torrents of dreams.

Roots

Roots, where are you?
Where Mama buried the sacred cord?
Cotton-spirit drifting on the wings of time,
seeds nourished by restlessness in black soil,
bearing fruits strewn across the earth.
Here today, there tomorrow, a songster traveler,
too short a season to love,
too long to feel the tear of leaving,
each anchor lifted before it hooks the nether depths.

Roots, where are you?
Is it at Mama's backyard
or in the nomad's back mind?
For these gold anchors never seem to hold long.

The Village Minstrel

If Akinwunmi had been a King
he would wear beaded crowns and gilded sandals,
dangle fly whisk of impostor authority,
decrees dripping fetid drivels
from his gold-toothed royal lips.
But he is only a Village Minstrel,
rendering lost lyrics of our forsaken beings.

If Omo Orosun had been a General
he would wear starched khaki suits,
carry swagger stick, adorned his spineless corps
with fake medals, tight leather belt with
silver buckles on cynical bloated paunch.
But he is only a Village Crier,
inspired by Mother Idoto's bard,
huge talking drum, never shutting up, never silenced.

If Akinsoji had been a politician, big government minister,
he would wear stiff agbada, beaded staff,
coral beads and dazzling gold chains, travel in
jets, limousines, Hummers bumping off
potholes dug for losers and lumpen
unfortunates on decrepit village roads.
But he is only a local school teacher,
frayed collars sowing hearts with wisdom seeds in parables.

If only Aremu had been a Bishop,
he would wear snow-white cassock, purple silk vests,
Savile Rowe suits. Carry pearl rosary, gold-plaited scepter.
Gold ring adorned, lofty throne on alien altar, holy Native
perched in Graceful surveillance of Diocesan plenty
amid neglected wants of dejected faithful.

But he is only an urban slum Jeremiah, heir to Isiah
endlessly lamenting as our people tell beads of sorrows.

Atinuke's son is no two-faced ruler,
Akingbade's scion is neither a purple-voiced
Bishop, nor torso-belted General. He is no
forked-tongued politician, sibling to pen-thief banker
converting the poor widow's mite to profit, tithes and bribes,
flying in private jets to redemption and paradise on earth.
He is only the Village Jester, market-square drummer,
town crier who sees more than he looks and hears more than is
said.

The Wanderer's Pulse

In Time

I. 1959

Blood splattered, fourth finger cut,
on the left side door of a Morris Minor.
At your shrine of rupture on Marina Jetty,
they offer hounds to the furnace and anvil Deity.
Betrayed wife, her tongue bitten bloody,
pride shattered, pain etched in inaudible incantations,
while nation half-awake dance in frenzy
to hopeful election beats,
heralding Independence promised.
Red, white and blue flag down,
green, white and green flag up.
Trouble mast planted,
burnt offerings to generations to come.

II. 1960

Birth pangs
that pain and blood deny,
happy parents' delight
as baby-nation cries,
a long-awaited birth announced.
Kith and kin dance as Union Jack down
swaddling cloth with no color black,
for an all-black nation born.
Joy, hope, dreams, fears unspoken, stream
the green, white, green skies and clouds
chanting tunes of ambition and fortune
yet unstained by the dirty oil lucre and spills.
Heady moments of vision and soaring dreams,
a people's will to fulfill, a land to enrich, a world to unchain,
generations to free, this child-land of yet-to-fill promises,
this Moses-led land without its Joshua for our times.

III. 1966

Five Majors, one General, one Colonel,
one crocodile totem that ate the unwary Poet.
A tale of leaders who met fiery death unprepared,
as young unknown soldiers taste first blood shed to cleanse,
later congealed as damnation in
their rites of passage of the beguiled.

Partakers of the lust that scorched this oil-soaked soil
with freedom songs of hate,
that devour generations,
break ancient bonds of trust,
betray pacts of sibling solidarity,
to welcome the reign of the firing squad.

They gave birth to carrion feeders
in seasons of fresh and stale blood,
spilling their collective curse on all of us,
a toxic waste that refuse to rot,
the perpetual ulcer in our national gut.

IV. June 12, 1993

Young soldiers of our misfortune
now blood-stained grown-ups.
Again, throttled our young nation's tender throat
in daylight pillage. Ugly naked power wearing
khaki drills, camouflage fatigues, belts and bullets
strut our streets, their soiled boots on our collective destiny.
New chains once more, on an abused, bewildered nation
these bearers of the blood-curse of 1966 stab old wounds,
that continue to gush pus from the nation's soul.

V. 2007

Gnarled fish-bone stuck in my throat year.
Stubborn chokes that strangled me.
Giant morsels of Ugaali and liters of water
all impotent wrestlers of this python hold
that all oil therapy defy.

Dark moments I would erase but in hot memory
recall the day that Mount Kenya burned, Kisumu roiled,
Lake Nakuru boiled over, Nairobi exploded, ancient
Rift Valley roared tremors of death
burying children, mothers, fathers, livestock
in fiery torrents of hate flooding farms,
fields, towns, homesteads and shanties.
CNN cackled at renewed tales of African "savagery"
streaming tragic scenes of unwanted bloodshed,
gleeful reels of angry lost youth roiling
across fragile theaters' fraudulent stage, crimson soaked.

Once again, the poor is fodder as Kenya burns,
Kenyans die in maize and flower farms,
Sugar cane, tea and coffee plantations,
city shanties and ranches all in flames
lit by greedy warlords touting injuries and historical grievances,
Land stolen, grabbed, seized, and invaded
fanning emotions of all sorts, twisted and boiling,
in this year of the gnarled fish-bone stuck in my throat,
choking grips that ease not as beautiful Kenya burnt.

VI. 2008

With Obama, Michelle, Jesse, and Al
we danced, cried sweet tears and rejoiced
that cold Chicago victory night
sprayed in fountains of light
pearls of joy glittering our renewal,
recovery, rediscovery and reckoning.
Reclaiming hope even as we tremble with fear,
nervous hearts beat mindful drums thumping memories
that reaction regroups, privilege fights back.
repression resents celebrations of emancipation.
But for now, our dreams we relish, our liberated
self-confidence we enjoy. We keep faith and forever hold firm
to promises the journeys to liberty never end.

VII. 2013 – *Westgate Nairobi*

Teach me the depths of your sorrows
that its pain silently grunts,
draped in masts of a different memory,
of glimmer, glitter and gold threads of sweat.
As beautiful people buy beautiful things
that betrayal and guilt assuage,
goods that wealth and glory's arrival trumpet.

Teach me the decks and decks of gloss in bright display
as some of us perfume our work-drenched bodies,
our exhausted breaths freshened and brightened
to give all the smiles of labor forced and willing.
Hired to clean, shine, sell, guard, hype and display
all now that with our blood and gore cruelly sprayed
on the day that all we sought was our daily bread
but found horror in full stride and roar,
rampaging cluttered aisles faith and lies demanding.

Teach me, I beg all who also suffer
the slow daze of an unfolding understanding
explaining why the Devil was let loose at the Mall.

Teach me the cries, soundless but deep
for Poet Baba Awonoor, for rich and poor,
for child and adult slain, Food Court turned butcher's slabs,
dance steps that tripped ripped bodies to graveyards.

Teach me, the smell, fears and tears that ooze
from layers of throttled selves of living and lifeless tangled,
fragrances of jasmine, cordite-blended at this spa of death.

Teach me the wideness beneath and beyond,
the grim debris of greed, hate and deceit
smothering grace, forgiveness and hope
dimmed lamps that light the future of terrorized lands
carried by the unsung, unscented that die and die not.

Teach me, teach me, I beg teach me.

VIII. 2020

Showers of fear seed the gray clouds,
showers of sorrow drench the chalky earth,
showers of anxiety
spout bleak bleached isolation,
flowering distance-masked suspicion
fed by orange-paté-led plots of mass denial
leafy covers for our red hot pain
washed in greasy soapy water.
Mists of death, misery and resignation
smother all in deathly gasps for air
hovering above Earth's spreading graveyard.

Prince and pauper swept in bristling icy waves,
healers, prophets, dancers and sage drowning,
trades, banks, crafts and markets swallowed.
Though profits of seven lives magically thrive in tech oases
in this year of the war of the invisible foe,
gliding in legion droplets of fear,
floating on icicles of sorrows,
hiding in swirling clouds of anxiety,
scourge to family and friendship bonds.
This familiar Ashetani in new attire
sweep leaders and followers into dank holes.
We waited and prayed,
for the savior pinpricks to deter the foe,
eyes closed, we endure pain pricks with prayer and tears,
pain pricks to abort pain, prayer to salve fear.
Finally, we danced, cried, clapped and laughed
in subdued joy, guilt-filled release, naked gratitude
as voices, songs, sighs, horns and tears of hope
ululate, croon with riffs and beats ushering the exit of 2020.

Places

I have lived Nairobi,
grown up in Lagos, matured in Dakar,
seen Delhi, felt Mumbai,
chilled at the Cape, contemplated Chennai,
respected Rio, cautious in JoBurg,
studied in London, rocked Brighton,
worked and dreamt in New York.

In New Orleans
I return to find rhythms
Katrina could not destroy,
blues and Jazz laced with Bourbon.
Kampala affirms home dreams,
red rain-drenched soil, mystery banana groves,
triumphant graves for Idi Amin's tomfoolery.

Dar, Mombasa, Maputo, Calabar, Cape Coast,
all blow breezes of genteel decay,
colonial pasts oozing coastal fish fragrance.
Hanoi's mopeds, suicide-paced sweep the Long Bien,
their siblings far away, floating in elegant boubous, perched
dazzling traffic-tease, Ouaga's Swagger-Amazons on two
wheels.

Onitsha market, confusion loose on web-toed Niger River,
Abidjan modern market for wars and wares
of sweet-bitter fruits of contested cocoa pods,
taunting ancient dry Niger town, Bamako.
But never in my life have I heard so many souls
whisper their entombed cries across generations,
as those lodged in layers by the Nile in Cairo.

Dakar

Here all the Signares of Saint Louis
a home true, theirs all theirs, finally found.
Stomping their swagger to rhythms natural
that with silver blue swirling sea waves, winds
dry and gritty crackling from the desert north
give you the many Gods, deities and Mammon
migrating from Rome, Mecca, Touba, Kaolack.
Love, passion, beauty, noise and arguments here
choreographed in troupes that artfully waltz
Cheikh Anta Diop's imagined Egypt, worlds made
in heritage to the race's proud bloodline
that keep this city confident, singing, dancing,
thinking, remaking the lonely defiant philosophy
that define and redefine our continent
defying the dirt, dust, dross, din of overwhelming
poverty, want, disease while overflowing with hope.
Here, freedom's muscles in elegance flex.
Here, stories in coral beads are told:
Beads of prayers tell our lives,
beads of sweat glisten our brows,
beads of honor crown our heads,
beads of beauty jiggle our waists,
beads of pride adorn our ankles.

Kampala

Pearl beads on a maiden nation,
your hills dance in graceful slow motion
to winds and clouds that gently caress
valleys of banana groves on shores of the Great Lake.
On red soil memory mounds, you ponder the many
stories, sad and sweet, of empires and kingdoms
buried in blood and gore on hands and hearts
of kings, false emperors, freedom fighters turned landlords.
Backs bent with weights of guilt, grunts of abomination
unmentionable in the tongues of the deities and ancestors,
your spirits groan under alien traditions imposed,
a lineage birthed by Lord Lugard with too many present-day
strutting heirs.
Your national spirit struggle as it reenacts martyrdom across
generations,
reclaiming shrines for saints of power, faith and want.
Home of the red earth, abused, you thrive, never giving up,
your maternal pride solid, receiving on your bosom child,
woman and man,
wounded, tired, mutilated in body, soul and mind,
their cruel cuts you heal, thirsty souls from endless journeys
you water.
Hope and forgiveness deep in scarred hearts you again inscribe.
Child bride nation, Spirit mother, pain and pleasure you
equally bear,
gathering your many children, saints, sick and wayward to
your bosom.

Addis Impressions

Shorthorns and shoe-shine boys,
donkeys, beggars, police men and revolutionary
guards all stern, olive city folks, all in rowdy mix
with peasants crossing regulated streets.
Pines in rows, beasts of burden, party flags,
an unending martial drill bearing history's symbols
in rituals, orthodoxies of order in regimes and rulers
across periods and places – Emperor, Marxists, Liberators,
pretenders of all hue feeding the people on promises false and
half true tales of conquests and wars,
fables that trumpet national and racial pride,
creeds that breed exclusive destiny above other African kin and
kith.
Ethiopia, ancient pride, honor and mythology magnified,
a necessity today in our continent long denied its history's
value, glory and respect.

Uppsala

What sons of Lot's wife full of rebellious Viking
Spirit, sneaking a mischievous backward glance,
must have committed this sin turning all within sight
into this pillar of salt, icy froth and smokes of chill?
Roads, roofs, rivers, railways and runways,
pillars, posts, pavilions, parks and plains,
fields, forests, factories, firms and farms,
gardens, garbage, garages, gates and galleries
all draped in blanket iciness.
The morning sun in dazzling boldness
breathe down searing flashes of brightness,
magic wands conjuring hot silver rays
cascading defiant slices of light into the frigid days,
offering deceptive moments of hope,
fleeting, sly conspiratorial winks to us wrapped up
smart sorry mummies seemingly braver
in our busyness than grizzlies, weavers and beavers
who in sensible hibernation burrow at home.

Cairo

I have in my heart many times
tried to truly return to this gilded City
of noise, beauty, guilt, history and imperial arrogance,
where trapped noble ancient spirits denied their
true selves for centuries in sealed concrete tombs
finding no rest seven thousand years later
scream fiery protests across ages, times and places
to pretender royal heirs of races, cultures, blended creed
whose rule history rewrite, pervert, drench and re-color
in diverse martial relayering and remembered
in adulation to often cruel conquerors across ages.

Here blows sandstorms of prejudice and pride,
ill wind that woman, Jewish, Nubian, Bedouin,
Copt, African black spare not. Shouts of "Abdi"
cultural and mercantile condescension, tone deaf
salutations accompany my journeys as soul-connections I seek
with mutual ancestry, universal identity but contempt meet,
as deluded people in national fundamentalist crypts entombed,
lock my human self in discredited memory of lost glory,
defunct kingdoms seeking to reclaim servitude, exploitation
and slavery,
heritage of trans-Saharan humiliation, pain and domination.
A sordid history I was never part of or ever want to be.

The Cape of Whose Hope?

On your coveted waterfronts of prosperity
I relive the tongues, lives, beliefs of Africa's long-suffering
ever-forgiving and trusting peoples of many soils.
Here I breathe cherished hopes of liberation
swept in by cold-warm waves of Siamese oceans
bonded in storms of tongues, beliefs and creed,
race and color that both enrich and deprave our humanity.

Yes, here I see ancient heritage lost and reclaimed that mold
these shores in authentic hybridity and legions of demons
that haunt the black, white, amber and more tapestry of your
destiny.
Inland, your magician-founders conjure anger, despair and pain
in Flats and dreaded townships, Harare reclaimed in
Khayelitsha's icy cold violence,
a perpetual winter in your people's summer hearts
enduring forced separation, legalized humiliation to hose for
others this fertile land of proud vine yards and arrogant stately
homes.

Cape of What Hope, good or vile?
On your shores I meet again
ancestral spirits across borders: healers, scholars, translators,
warriors, rock artists, carvers, diviners, star-gazers of antiquity.
Pioneer gifter of the foreigner his voice in Ajami script, form
new, yet ancient, though opaque to race-blinded imperial eyes.

Cape of Whose Hope?
Here remains the stench of banishment, lynching, exile,
poor people's gun smoke isolation in Apartheid's colored silos
self-violating for crumbs from the privileged Table Mountain.

The Mahatma at Tavistock Square

In your quiet recess,
in oblivion of the screeching intellectual struts
that the Square at Bloomsbury often evoke
cloisters and towers that have lost luster and peace,
in these sacred greens, I find my Ashram
with neither labels nor strictures
deep in a defunct Empire's heart,
a city that once ruled the world.

I find disciples displaced, despised, depressed,
candles lit, incense burning, rice sprinkled to wayward pigeons'
delight.
I find meditations, penance, intercessions for a world mired in
hatred, prejudice, war and greed under scions of the rulers you
once fought.

In this graveyard at Tavistock Square
I find a weird peace, a haven, a shrine without the urn, shroud,
or ash already sprinkled in the Nile at Jinja.

On this memorial to the Sage Saint
where the knowing few tread in studied reverence,
the many in ignorance and sincere indifference,
their dogs leashed and loose, some minds lost,
their smiles glazed in joys of ecstasy obtained not too far away
from the dealers at King's Cross Station.

In your interim peace and stillness, we all inhale fumes
of a world of gods of incessant motion, rush and noise.

Dreaming on Sherbrooke Street, Montreal

(While waiting for Adiaha)

On floating aromas, deep brown black,
in traditional coffee shops you drink
deep of contentment, of what you want to be.
Shut out sad newsreels of today's reality
glide on wings of inspiration on Sherbrooke street.
In Montreal's freezing November midday you drill
with Ian Banks the imagination of mystery
sipping weak coffee awaiting Adiaha's return.

In black and white, silver and gold you still dream.
Dreaming is the breast stroke across the world's waves,
the deep plunge into seas, clouds and skies,
transported by story tellers, strummers of canvas,
lyricists of sound and color, subtle intruding scent
of dry leather, green leaf, fresh rain dark earth,
brown and damp fertile wombs of mystery and beauty,
modern and ancient engraved on a mental disk in our digital
age.

First Impressions at Nairobi Fashion Show, 1985

High class fashion parade
privilege, pride, style and glitter
in glass and gold massive theater.

Beauties of all races
glide across the stage in grace
dressed in fashion from all places.

We breathe perfumed purified air
sprayed by bedraggled waiters
wearing stained and ill-fitting attire.

Meanwhile our big men of all races
in reserved seats of finest comfort and leather
enjoy to the fullest the ongoing sweet weather.

We watch the show installed on
rows of streets conveying powerful names,
Konainge Street, Kenyatta Avenue, Oginga Odinga Street.

And behind us, Kimathi, a memory of dread
wildness forcibly remembered, guilt-laden close
to the "Emergency Exit" and other conveniences.

As for the Leader, moments in executive stands,
faces on bank notes that proudly say
'L'État? C'est Moi,' isn't it?

As the show rolls on,
workers, teachers, peasants in their millions
in farms, firms and schools in sober procession
sing the multi-tongued Uhuru,
wondering if Ugaali and Sukuma wiki
on the table is better, no matter the leader?

Upper Hill Nairobi Frieze

Misty cold morn blues
Chorus Mount Kenya dew droplets
Mid-air hanging invisible flakes stringing
Icy scents that unwilling bodies adorn
Sensitive musty nostrils clogged.
Towers of light and waters, vapor drapes
Spraying showers on silver
Skylines dancing in step with the hills of Ngong.
Frames that make me wonder, ponder and again wonder
A global warmth that my waking day resolve freezes.

Land of the Rift, Lakes and Mountains

Ancient land of ours
artery of the forests and snake river
in the heart of the Rift's hallowed plains, cold and hot,
dry, verdant valleys of mountains that thunder
rain, clouds and snow, bejeweled caps of ice that nourish
thirsty lands in deep blue lacustrine pools, inland seas
ancient witnesses to all our ancestors conception.

Beautiful land of ours
home of Nature's lean harsh allure
seeded by heaven's tongues of fire
birthing life's unequaled glorious music
symphonies played in black, brown and white
that flowed up and down the Nile's imperial waves.

Bounteous land of ours
collision scenes today for game and human
under Kilimanjaro's towering icy masts
now rivaled by man's satellite toxic towers.
Once God's abode in pools of royal lakes
dripping soothing relief to the ancient Horn's
long parched and dry cunning tongue.

Colorful land of ours
volcanic clefts that sprang Adam's children
spewed across earth's vast terrain
inventing creeds and greed, colors and tongues
that nations, parties and kings create
to divide humankind, exploit and dominate.

Mysterious land of ours,
legends of defunct races, imagined ancestry,

breeding today's pain, hate and death,
tales of Nilotes, Hamites, Semites and Bantu,
brown, white, black and in between, grafts
of the first stirrings in a dry Rift womb.

Unforgettable land of ours
habitat for beings all types, carnivores, herbivores,
spectacular crossings compelled by Nature
into lands emptied of people and love, pawns
in imperial project to freeze beauty and cruelty
for the delight of the tourist paying few.

Memories of Breakdown Camp

Mothers and fathers we learned to be
in the early and cold hours between
dawn and morn when mom and dad
fought, loved, then played lovers
in groans, bites, scratches, sobs and curses,
gropes and embrace behind tattered curtains
just before Dad into the early morning rush plunge.
Gates to open, lawns to tend, mansions
and grounds to watch in company of guard dogs,
stray monkeys that raid orchards, black kites
in search of prey, defiant baboons lost in town.
Dad, a faceless man in soulless chore
spirit bruised, body scratched, sore,
worn out as his frayed brown overalls,
a slave labor to plunderers of our commonwealth.
Father comes home hollowed out, mind drowned
in poison fumes of Changaa, limbs
that his wounded spirit drags iron-weighted, a life
angry and bruised, the mad street dog trapped for slaughter,
awaiting offerings of the oppressed who in pain
and humiliation explode scattering shrapnel on loved ones.

Tourist Attraction at Namanga

Brown red black lined cloth pieces,
tonged, tied, draped in flowing ease
body adorned with rings, pins and piercings.
Proud, wild warrior satiating your cravings
with knives, clubs, spears, swords and tales
inventing wilderness, noble native savage rare,
our payback for your wanton plunder,
gory exploitation, worldwide destruction
as you today delight and overflow with joy
at real warriors of primordial times, beads, knives,
clubs and all. Yes, clubs and cubs you celebrate,
lion hunts, tourist conquests, smooth and uncut
clubs unprotected, seeding viruses, offspring denied.
Your jungle the fever, heat and drool, drive
from military and celebrity tours as you
claim trophies and scalps of different hues,
worship upright heights that kiss the skies,
your dreams and hopes you get and more;
purple and white sashes, Manyattas and Kikoys,
enchanting smiles breathed from gap-toothed faces
promise, peril, adventures and myths laden
as dry dusty ill-winds of the plains of the damned
we escape, brewing mixed realities of tribesman,
native, post-modern artist of the slippery pot
that hold futures, present and past, the lot.
Educated as all, in love, trade, power and war
smokescreens of illusions conjured in mourning
for ancestral lands, memory daily lost and sold in pain.

Now They Hawk Spittle!

Have you seen Sibonelo?
As you pass by the marketplace
near the township Taxi Stage where dung hills grow?

Have you seen Sibonelo,
gaunt son of dead warrior, now a beetle
seeking squalor glory in urban decay?

I hear he now sells saliva to the white man's Sangoma!
Globules of spit, deadly droplets, carriers of killer life
stronger than sperm, for the laboratory's use.

While others hawk their blood and kidney
Sibonelo, Lord of all scavengers coughs blood and phlegm,
He coughs and spits for his thirty pieces of silver.

Merry Me Tonight

I work internationally,
fly night and day, sleep casually,
beds on rigs, hotels and bush stations.
I make change happen, get justice done,
make money work for rich and poor,
build banks and bridges,
engineer plants and seeds,
connect the world Wi-Fi and cell,
keep fragile peace, war wounds heal.

I am John, international John!
Weary change-maker, here so forlorn,
bone-cold lonely in your Babylon.
In drinks and caffeine, I find joy,
seek love in supine embraces hot
ensnared by your laser green shy glances.
So, drink from my alien bounty pool
my Cleopatra, my low hanging fruit,
my Jezebel, star in my sultry tinted torpor.

Eat, drink and merry me tonight.
My bride price is Sterling, Euro and Dollar.
Pardon my lack of graces, tipsy swagger,
desperate rush to close the deal, your name,
age and creed ignored. I see the lurking Madam,
the preening pimp, sneaky concierge,
all your pound of flesh waiting to be carved.
Your svelte mystery, black pidgin modernity
in hot dark passion waves drown me.

Let's not talk tonight about
Genocide in Darfur, slavery in Nouakchott,

rape in Bukavu, hustling in Korogocho,
mutilation in Gulu, despair in Cape Flats.
Let's rave tonight, make merry and enjoy,
do what Europe forbid, America abhor,
faiths condemn, all secretly covet.
Let's the virus dare, the germs taunt,
sink all in surrender at this Aphrodite's haunt.

The Wanderer's Pulse

Come,
wander with me the chambers of my soul
through the starry fortress of my spirit,
stills and motions where thought and emotions
meet past in present in sighs and songs.

Come,
let us tour the inner shrines of my being
along deep corridors of wood and gold,
home to the drift and shifts,
lights on the walls of my life's gallery.

Come,
swim with me the seas of my dreams,
deep and calm running waters
from which I sip and float
springs of doubt and faith.

Come,
let us soar on the wings of my hopes,
skies and heights seeded with fears defied,
gliding on clouds in elated flight,
one eye on the depths beneath.

Come,
feel my wanderer's pulse,
throbs from my innermost being,
strums from unending moments of astonishment,
music to an enduring striving that is living.

Lagos and New York

Deadlines

Despair, the Lagos mob's necklace
cruel, my chest, weight invisible
press down. In gasoline sweat
my being drenched, day time nightmare,
strange ghosts and demons my inner
self haunt as with deadlines I battle
spinning my creative lines dead, unburied,
their paths woven in my creation famine,
shuttles of fixated endless refinements
in this cold land of summers' unbearable
heat that my brain fries, my day drains,
but sure I am that Skye's commission in due
time will be finished, my salvation without
an army certain, my promise to redeem true.

Early Morning Hustle at Makoko's Waterfront

It is early morning,
drunk with purpose we rise
set against the cloudy tides
of the day's sluggish unfolding.

We set our dug-outs to the lagoon
our nets frayed, stretched taut.
Into the deeps we toss again and again
our everyday hope for the huge catch
dreamt of in last night's restless sleep
but only filled with today's morning empty promise.

Our boats we row on along our day's endless deeps
turned shallows with sawmill and sewage waste. We
still search in vain for the wealth buried in the dross,
stuck in our deepest resolve in the storms of daily busyness.

We are drenched
as our battered canoe weaves,
turns, bobs and tosses in this City's perilous straits
where all that matters to our worn-out souls fail.

Message from Mount Isolo Dump

One day this city will sink
under its weight of plastic
in suffocating grip on its grimy neck
wrapped like a mummy in perpetual filth.

One day this city will crack
from dynamites of seething anger
buried in boiling hearts of deprived youth
in scattered pieces of exploding might.

One day this city will drown
in endless humiliation
released by vicious leaders in their urge
to drench us in foul oppression.

One day this city will raise
fresh morning scent in glory and triumph
on wings of work, hope and love
that ordinary folk crave and pray.

A Stout Brewed at Ikeja

What in that black brew made at Ikeja
did the old Irish mix that made you rue
the day your palate was so helplessly wooed?
Potent world conqueror, empire
greater than Her Majesty's forced dream,
stouter than the rugby Lions, a winner in love and soccer.
Adored criminally cold or room temperature warmth,
her faithfuls in these torrid and dry climes of ours
swear by its unalloyed herbal healing power.
This trickster transvaluer of black power quality,
an all-consoling warmth provider,
fragrant-pleasing and acceptable to the gods,
transporting believers at our communion hour,
lips twitching, body shaking, in reverent anticipation,
sober submission in fear at the promise
of power, vitality, elation, stupor and inebriation.

Frank and Company at Bogobiri

What manner of Frank is this
at Bogobiri corner installed
the famous stout brew nursing
whose witch's recipe I decipher not?
But in my ancestors' true Santeria traditions
cigar smoke spewing he disperses
all evil spirits black, white and brown.
Baba Aladura at his night's worship,
Doubters and believers congregate
offering interactive homilies on bosses in Lagos,
amputees in Freetown on rhythmic crutches,
anger, sorrow and pain spiking the ground,
every step a condemnation of Africa's leaders
whose nests, blood jewels feather.
Frank's court at Bogobiri,
open shrine for wily fraudsters, angry intellectuals,
cunning laggards and jazz lovers in communion with
news hounds, village clowns, singers yet to find their voices.
At Bogobiri, there's place for all and sundry,
There's place for art and farce!

From Kakadu to Kalakuta

(For Fela Anikulapo Kuti)

To life rather than death
we drank ourselves high at Kakadu,
smoked and clapped with the Chief Priest,
trumpet, clarinet and sax, a new world, brave
and sweet, sounds and rhythms opened
our beings to worship and adore.
Drum beats, strums that talk to taste buds unusual,
unknown, unreal, unearthed by Baba Allen.
Afro-jazz turned Afro-beat, liberation songs
in ancestral beats found on electric piano,
guitars, tambourines, mother drums that boom
across ten distant villages and crowded Lagos City.
Voice and sonorous rhythm deep and compelling
ancestral spirits to rise, join the celebration of the living
in festivals of worship and convocation that affirm life,
demand freedom, reclaim history, revive our souls
beyond the repression of "Authority Stealing",
the "Unknown Soldiers" and crony bloody civilians
that plunder our nation, defile our destiny,
blight the future and hope of our multitude young.
Bass riffs, strong chorus, defiant dance moves, freedom songs
in smokes sent up to the heavens daily announce
Abami Eda's vision, art, fight and sacrifice at Kalakuta.

Mouths Are Made for Better Things...

(Memories of Ajele Cemetery at Campos Square, Lagos,
Nigeria)

All our dead died long before the Colonials
moved the cemetery far from the City center,
Ghosts laid to writhe in suburban bush heat
that native slums from Colonials separate.
Government Reservation Areas for white-skin rulers,
tongues perched on hot stones
spitting words through slit nostrils.

Mouths they say are made for better things
like eating chicken whole but not the bones,
feet, head, wings, all sweeter parts
except bits that the village gossip turns you,
"God forbid bad thing", tongue all loose
restraint all gone, every one's secrets revealed.

Mouths they say are made for better things
like smoking lavender-flavored pipe tobacco,
blue fumes chasing evil spirits.
The colonialists spoke through their noses,
heard with their eyes, meanings sketched
in ethnography books, exotic tales of savage lore,
tribal moods on canvas that denied recognition,
understanding, wisdom, intelligence, our knowledge deride.
The cemetery they moved, bodies and bones they left
homeless spirits to haunt our native souls at Ajele.

But recalcitrant youth, forerunners of Area Boys,
turn tombs to couch beds and love nests where we sat,
gambled, smoked weed, sang, danced and dared
evil spirits their heads raise if they can.

Here women and strangers travel escorted
across this dead cemetery of the forsaken dead.
We are the only demons that walked the daylight
the spirits that rode the wings of the night
boys and men who the Colonizer's Hades colonized.
Even now our masquerades speak through their noses
voices of the dead that haunt the living, now we know
mouths have always been made for better things.

In New York City

From each city new and old
its own voice, its own music hot and cold
New York City sings me its own
Lagos City drums a different town.
New York City sings to me
in whispered croons amidst
life's unruly noises, dust, hurry and smog
shining light on my anthill life down and up
ceaseless motion of duty, doing and work.
These cities smiles a pace, a space, hidden place of heart
where I shower in deep thoughtful joy and mirth.

Mara Sunset in Manhattan

I see the Mara
in Manhattan's skylight
drops of gold dust brightening the sky
amidst blankets of floating gray
atop seas of khaki plains smog-drenched,
years of grind of the sad many unknowns
for the greed, drink, smoke, and mischief
of the few in luxury, luck and birthright.

I see the Serengeti sunset dip
in this land, gray, dark, dim and contrived
where many and more are playing the wild
beyond the jungle and plains of my imagination
sunrise and sunset on roof tops of my mind,
coffee aromas to the chippings of the new day,
beef broth froth dulling the cricket cries
of nature's retreat for toilers of the day
wake up calls for all laborers at dusk.

Mara sunrise lights the deeps
within my yearning soul transported
heights beyond this ever-alien dreamland
where endless lamps light up ordinary joys,
Christmas and all festive moments trumpeted in drapes,
drips, drones of rainbow colors skies
mimicking the brightness of life lit gold in short days,
life trapped by Adam's curse, a spiritual quarrel
still unresolved, an everlasting hole in our human soul.

A Cock Crows Outside My Window

Yes, a cock crows
outside my window,
seventy-seven floors up,
all glass and concrete,
by the East River.
I hear a cock crow,
not once, not twice but thrice
as my daily wage slave I deny
in affirmation of my free humanity.

I hear a cock crow
at dawn in my head,
in my heart, my being
as every morning's mists.
Another day's drought in souls dare
with cockcrow ringing, beckoning.
Timid tired selves arise on a new day's
many trails, trials, travails and triumphs.

Adventures and routine boredom clacking,
Screeching wheels, wailing brakes, train
Station crush, subway rush, children's school's
Hassles, chores, work place sore rash
Anxieties sprayed by hollowed out bosses,
Filled with the sour stench of their lifelong neuroses.

Yes, a cock crows
outside my window.
Atop the dawn's traffic riot,
drill and din, dross and dirt,
morning construction cacophony, confusion
orchestrated in bad tempered symphonies.

I hear a cock crow
on my window sill,
sunrise greeting cheerily,
welcoming a new morn's mirage,
as we charge the red daze of our day's unjust dessert.

Fields of Jersey Along the Rail Tracks

Greenery that green fields displace,
tall grim grasses straddling slimy waters,
shale-brown orange-brick rail tracks
with banks bathed gray-dim.
Jersey to Penn Station in grime
display swamps, oil-slaked, wildlife
diminished, imitating fields drab and dross.
Pillars dark-stale rust stand head-bowed
at stain of earth and land wounded,
reminders of enterprises that waste
places, spaces, waters and fields.

Manhattan Mists

Manhattan,
joyful irreverent noises along Broadway.
Jams and slams, rap and dance,
operas, ballets, musicals and jazz
play emotions and motions, all hues,
sweat, color, light and love
of this hybrid bounty.

Manhattan,
hearts beat ceaselessly to work,
People sleepwalking
in the gray-gold East River dawn.
This city killed sleep, blaring
Lyrical insomnia, conjuring
Twin Towers' dirge into resurrection hymn.

Manhattan
Thousand alien tongues singing
Discordant commercial harmony
Defying WASP's cultural Babel
Your custom, royal claimants, they beckon
Selling you things you neither thought you needed nor wanted.

A Reflection in the Hudson

In luxury leather, fiber glass, shiny steel,
silver eagle, above the Hudson, we soar.
Floating the blue sky mile high, on wings we
breach gray blue clouds that embrace
warm diamond thousand arrows. Uncountable
droplets of electric lights below, purple and orange
fireflies that tease as we pierce the sun,
caressing warmth to the gray old Lady Liberty,
stout and stately in Atlantis-mirrored splendor.
Shimmering Madonna in glittering dance sway
atop bejeweled mermaids in glass cases.
The wonder and mystery roil, overwhelm,
as this pearly illusion swirls its multiple images.
Harbors and homes, bridges, roads and rails,
streets and schools, parks, trees and lakes,
firms and factories, flora and fauna, zoos
embalmed in this massive pearl-gold aquarium.
What dreadful beauty?
What astonishing glittering spectacle?
What if all these were true!

Anonymous in New York

Unknown
I thrive
in your gray-silver anonymity
your concrete and glass jungle I navigate
lush, stunted trees and twigs in
stubborn oases, dog-manure
nourished, domains to desperate lonely
birds in cohabitation with humans equally
isolated as the birds tweet their new-found joy
unlike the city people's sweaty rage.

Unseen
I drift
unmarked wind-swept cotton fluff
floating by museums, galleries, church
aisles, underground station crowds, melting
my way sniffing olive cloud smokes
of tough cigar-totting jazz club bouncers.
Twenty-first century shadow spirit, invented
authentic self in multiple copies, stealing
invisible pleasures my hungry eyes feed endlessly,
epicure of the countless sounds, scent and sight.

Unheard
I blend
into softly strummed solitude
with cranks and crooks swaying
the silver-edged gauntlet running
in this Everyman crowded city.
Eyes forever down, I count dusty
shoes, frayed heels, loud tired vein
trunks, forbidden by your unspoken
norms, to make eye contact with the other.

The Immigrant's Laments

On tip toe, hole-in-socks, we tread
in terror of dreaded acronyms
that seek papers faked or lacked.
Papers brought us here, dreams in green
currency, diploma, visas from poverty and pain
to free us from creeping gripping horror
that entire families, communities devour.
Modern-day refugees we flee, drifting here
to these long-valued freedom shores
enacting bold and proud our own Mayflower.

Tethered to poles of predefined status, we live,
clouds of Amistad's history,
hostility noose on dark stranger necks,
as we dream the release generations
before us found in escape from chains,
that deny us our God to find and love,
our manners hard for nobility not so ancient
that burn the cross in sheets and hood rituals,
dangling ropes that dare curly heads raise
in pride, our humanity locked in frigid prejudice.

The streets we sweep, sleep we kill
for the almighty dollar. Bound by paper
that daily its value shift, in immersion
we plunge, our history and selves melting,
true to lines proudly recited by initiated
forerunners of treasures rare and enchanting.
In lives tough, harsh but deemed better, into new
waves of misery we dive self-transported to toil
as our paradise become the land to weep, our Babylon,
even if success is wealth that grew and swallowed us.

Enduring pain and abuse, our turn patiently
we await, bodies, souls wracked by menial misuse.
Branded by color and alien accents,
the stop search, and other humiliation
provoke our spirits unbowed as we claim
our rights denied not because of failed humanity
but guilt-wounded hearts that refuse to heal,
demanding passive submission and erased memory
as residency titles for a propertied pecking order
an inglorious endowment to injustice in perpetuity.

Waves on City Streets

Coffee shop on city terraces
become the high rocks of the beach
as tides of humans slowly wash by,
dogs, their poo and all types of baggage in tow.
Astonished, light of my mind switch on
Glancing at populations sweeping by,
waves of humans in uneven roar and motion,
bearing waste, taste, treasures, tension, and tears.

Swimmers too few I see here, many more drifters
in perpetual go-with-the-flow known and unknown,
floating on all powerful sweeps and shifts, direction
hidden. But divers too I see, brave and bold, daring
all in deed and spirit, as they plunge dressed
for occasions their own making in life's deep seas,
turbulent, cruel, sharp and icy terrains
of thrills, feels, kills, ills and ease found together.

Lady Liberty's Promise?

On paved streets neutered hounds populated,
pearl sweetness of generous smiles to many
I learn not to foolishly squander,
as in isolated cracks of brick-layered earth elusive joys I sniff
in multi-formed reality tales told, many colored
sounds and sights. Solid strolls, mental maps drawing,
the giant soul of this city inscribes itself on my mind.

This land built on equal opportunity sweat, muscle,
blood and tears from whose depths the long ago holler
songs of African spirits echoing in flourish of blues,
jazz, gospels on soils washed East and West by rivers
streaming imperial boundaries of glass, gold and steel,
dreams and ambitions that scrape skywards, endless
glory towers built, imagined beyond gory island fortress
prisons and spiked walls. Grim monuments, daily memory
for the many gullible lives drifting along: the naive, the misled,
the wayward and the unfortunate that Lady Liberty in her
stern glory, promise not only glamour, grandeur and freedom
but also gaol, gallows, graves and woes on Riker's Island.

The Mouride Spirit in Manhattan

Young Cheikh calls me Pops,
glistening teeth and warm smiles
as due diligence shopping I do
on late Friday evenings, walking aisles
filled with goods, excess luxuries
for bloated and selfish consumption.
On different wings of Mouride worlds
work, school, industry, trade and faith
soar Young Cheikh, lawyer-to-be,
in stores and factories working, night
on sidewalks and squares of Fifth Avenue
with dad to trade, haggle and hustle.
Bags, scarves, watches, fake and genuine,
designer goods, all for sale in the spirit of enterprise
or is it capitalism long before Weber, Marx,
Schumpeter claimed enterprise for Europeans only.
Cheikh's community, in enterprise and faith
cross oceans, deserts, plains and mountains,
ride waves of deity and mammon, meet
Caesars, Sultans, Rajs and Republics too
for trade, profit and enterprise, Touba to build,
God to exalt, for Cheikh Bamba's children worldwide.

The Mugger in Me

There's a mugger in me,
more than two decades
of schooling, a man of the cloth,
with collar, rosary beads, crucifix
on a most pious and serene posture.
Past middle age, looking older, a serious,
friendly confident African adult.
All visible markers of the ever present
mugger in my grown black maleness.

There's a mugger in me,
scaring old ladies, making couples shiver,
As men climb mounts of chivalry to cover
their vulnerable females cowering behind solid male frames.
Blind to formal wear, mature looks, they quake
in dimly lit alleys as they await, my deadly
pistol and the hidden knife of the ever present
mugger in my black maleness.

Street Beggar Poetry

I did not buy friendship
with dollar bills, penance-soaked,
placed in expired Starbucks cups.

I did not buy friendship
with coins hurriedly dropped
eye-averting reply to a beggar's plea.

We built friendship's bridge
when stooping I asked him
about the many books on his laps.

I found a street wise man
proclaiming prophecies, Isaiah
demand-making in rhyme and verse.

I found street beggar poetry,
troves of street sense treasury,
Nietzsche and Langston Hughes inspired.

The Sage on 58th and First

Al is the sage
for whose wisdom we pay
our dollars bills.
For two minutes we buy interaction,
oiling our minds, salving our broken consciences.
We drop coins in plastic cups, into wishing wells
of a bi-polar mind and heart,
Cicero in need of a dental job,
Jekyll and Hyde's folly and wisdom,
reminder of traditions of yore
that kept priests, poets, fools and culture.

Street Sense Vibes

While lyrics and music
with coffee aroma jam
at The Orchard on 58th,
the diamond vibes, unalloyed
disguise from outside shine
at the corner on the floor,
there squats street wisdom, street rhymes.

Love for Dinner – Manhattan home-dining?

Tonight
we serve love for dinner
recipe plucked out from the TV
ingredients from the corner store:
chop, grate, crisp and well strained
cook and simmer, follow YouTube tips
closely, then glut ourselves on imagined
royal feast drowned in red wine.

Tomorrow
we serve romance for breakfast
recommended by pundits
mixed and mashed, grilled to taste
spiced and marinated, the media's way
fare defined by celebrity chefs.

For lunch
we get a quickie
sea food and vegetable quiche,
baked, light touch spiced seduction,
reality show squeezed in juicy emotions,
satiation for temporary lonely hearts.

Street Faces

They lost laughter,
dulled the glint that
smiled out loud burying it
under the weight of dung hills,
heavy anxieties blanketing souls.

They lost laughter,
killed the glow that shine
from hearts alive, thriving,
all smothered in suspicion,
endless hums in their heads.

They lost laughter,
wearing faces that shame
their many abused puppies,
chained on leashes of disgrace
to routine despair and boredom.

City Jungle

In the other on the street
I find other blood-soaked claws and fangs,
lone wolves worse than I.
Rogue buffalo, wary weary
on prowl on dog-poo side walks
sniffing out friendly-smile weakness.

In their red coal-fire eye
a perennial unknowing prey
I await the trap, a meek doe
caught in the chilling
glare of the leopards of the night,
the reward for unwary eye contact
in this jungle.

A Homeless Nomad's Moments

His home on his tortoise-back,
hard shell of wear and tear,
he carries on an overburdened cart.
Belongings bearing life that never
in one place or time belonged, an intense
nomad in spirit and restless being.
Life, for him a geography of minutes,
scenes, times and places in emotions,
moods, moments configured. Life moved,
enjoyed, treasured, suffered, died, lived.
Mountains climbed in thought and deed,
jagged peaks, snow-capped, beauty and might
in altitudes that provoke awe and sickness.
Twins in the feelings of moments.
He descends into valleys, grass plains,
green, rocks, deserts filled with human hyenas
stalking the fields and the city, man's angry arenas.

Beats on Politics

How Do We Sing a Song to Fifty Years in Dependence?

Our life's story plays, miles of twisted reels unfurled,
gold threads on this blood-soaked slippery theater.
The stage, a sculpted Eternity's crossroads
in shards of palm kernels and cowries engraved,
that spins labyrinths of false exits and entrances.

Moments unformed, unfinished, tattered wraps of our tales
unfold,
bearing phantom fetuses in history's dark womb,
seeds of two thousand seasons of wanton rape!
Descendants uncountable, soiled sands on our shores,
authoring multiple texts,
Babel's off-springs, spinners of confused fables.

Our multi-colored masques dance our dream,
"Ashetani", our tale's hero choreographs the raucous chorus,
multi-racial hermaphrodite, forked tongue mischief maker,
imp adorned in many colors, embedded in all creeds,
rainbow-child villain across many worlds.

Steeds of invented history skip across our stage
while our modern choir stutter their song:
"How do we trip a dance to fifty years in dependence"?
Under scions of slavers, thieving leaders, warrant chiefs and
rogue traders,
Askaris bedecked in fake medals, tear gas and cattle prods.

Our cast of heroes, villains, spirits and demons,
narrators who unmake history, defilers of our earth,
telling tales of the ugly ones, too many so far born,
plunderers of our collective fortune cursed by deities spurned,
bankrupt impresarios in this dim theater of our betrayal.

Our post-colonial chorus still sputters:
"How do we sing a joyful song to fifty years in dependence?"
Under misleaders that bury live bulls, virgin youth and straying
strangers,
smashing unformed skulls, sucking black gold and blood
in their unholy covenant that is our undying pain.

Their abomination our lot condemn to fifty seasons
of purgatory in wilderness of sorrow and want.
Souls adrift, spirits confounded, nation rudderless,
as we await our redemption's prophet-sacrifice,
bearer of our ultimate atonement and emancipation.

Our life story unfinished rocks our theater,
foundations quaking, curtains torn, moats cracked
as abused audience become actors taking center-stage.
For it is our time, we who defy death and claim life,
to toss our depraved bloated kings in the lion's ring!

Confessions at the National Altar

We come tainted with tar,
dry blood, stale tobacco stain
on calico drapes of wounded collective soul,
as the blunt knife stabs the national
heart with anguish swollen at so much loss.

We come tainted with guilt,
with pain, collective suffering
stoked by constipated bad leaders,
who stole from the shrine
offerings given for our well-being.

We come tainted petty,
no matter the individual laurels,
the victory struts of captains of
de-industrialization who beat their chests
with hands soaked in dyes of shameful complicity.

We come tainted ghoul,
even when we build mega-churches,
create financial empires,
establish foundations to alleviate poverty,
as long as our home is founded on shifting sands.

We come tainted blind,
from the perpetual glare of traffic lights,
stuck in amber, never changing, neither
turning green nor red for national goals
sworn to in billions of the nation's wealth.

We come tainted foul,
drenched in our national

he-goat stench, pontificating wisdom
to a world that winks and pokes,
knowing none is clean until all is clean.

We come fraud-tainted,
parents, citizens, believers all,
even our children believe no longer
as we rear them wallowing in our
new faith of cynical collective lie.

We will surely rise clean,
fresh-breath proud, glorious first-fruits,
the day in our national torment
that we seek total rebirth, renouncing
the ways of generations that wasted our lives.

Questions for the Ogas at the Top

You have to ask dry-rot scented leaders,
perennial blue-loined Vervet grooms,
despoilers of our national destiny
trapped in their darkened salons
what happened to our vital story?

You have to ask practiced senior liars,
khaki-starched necks,
leather-belted paunches,
gout and goitered Oga,
what happened to our songs of hope?

You have to ask blood guilty barons and chiefs,
slippery seekers after oil-rent,
choked on stale lobes of conscience,
connivers in betraying our future,
what happened to our golden dreams?

Provocateur-General

Honey-lipped, salt-tongued provocateur,
oily voice, sour breath, finality assured.
In mockery you ask of what use after all these years
of weary drummers their hearts pounding out?
Or town criers hoarse with screams of how
we live in the house of hunger and why at dawn
we must set forth. You gloat
demanding what profit is it that the Oracles
foretold lives just before dawn, or that things fall apart,
a people's life no longer at ease? You rejoice
that our beautyful ones are not yet born.
You scorn our griots, embrace sister kill joy,
deny our lofty dreams, applaud the darkness
of two thousand seasons without healers.
You taunt casualties shuttling in the crypt,
awaiting our man of the people, nation's voice
silenced, the road blocked, strewn with sad
petals of blood. In laughter your gong mocks
our dance of the forests deriding our journeys as
lives wasted on road famished, our gods...to blame!
But you lie General, colonial war-time porter
now local-royalty, Commander-in-Thief, national plunderer.
You mock too soon wily provocateur, this journey
is dreary, tiresome, long, painful but not final.
Its routes with many seasons and moons ahead,
its battles, crowns of victory promise, dance,
Songs unfinished, tales still richly unfolding.
Flaunt not your victor's swagger, prance, you may
but not yet in victory on our history's theater.

Season of Explosive Expectations

Tinder box society,
powder keg community,
lives on sharp edges skiting slippery downhill.
Daily realities exuding fumes of suffering,
dusts of hate, rays that blind virtue,
showers that spew sorrow and pain.
Terrains of thunders, floods, sandstorms, mud avalanches,
sinister siblings,
as drought stabs kinsmen
to famine's slow deaths.

Pregnant moments of peace deceive us all, untroubled
stillness, bearer of jinxed portents, the calm
before the mindless sudden bloody slaughter.
The dust and rubble mass burial in collapsed buildings,
the fury of the fiery mob's necklace.
Seasons of amputations, the militia's mission, Sharia's
retribution. The suicide bomber's last rites, screams
sending rivers, streams, lakes gushing murky, seething
waves of viruses, multiple plagues in our times.
Every red brown dust evening haze imbued
with crackles of crazed anger. Nature's rebellion
today, man's greed exploded yesterday. Tomorrow,
demented fundamentalists' cackles. Blind hot enmity
at other clan, creed and race. Mass human sacrifices,
altars of blood, our now daily unexpected routine
for us dwellers in this season of explosive expectations.

Biafran Homecoming

Biafra came home as bitter sorrows; kernel uncracked,
our own indigenes turned squatters on their own land,
neither compassion nor rent requited,
as victims are blamed for exile not so unforced,
ingrates that must thank mother nature for hoarded assets,
nature's gift in cassava tubers buried, bloated with riches
from generous blood-manured soil.

Biafra came home as woes remembered
bridges broken, shrines ruined, schools burnt,
teenage girls raped by all unknown soldiers,
souls wounded as parents simulate deadly pox
with daughters painted in ash and ocher spots, skin
discolored, while martyred mothers' bodies
tendered in sacrifice, unholy war front for cruel men.

Biafra came home as wounds unhealed,
dredged torrents of hope unrealized
no longer realizable, geography and gene
muddied with greed, deceit and despair
as the land, now oil-narcotized, terror-stricken,
weave lives, futures, expectations into concrete
knots, leaders and followers in sealed cement pods.

Biafra Seed

Planted on a fertile soil of imagined hope
choked by deceitful thorns and weeds,
this seed has failed to sprout and bear good fruit.
Sown on modern-day memory chip soldered
in dust, mold and grime, but live, so alive
Biafra, lives in many unsure minds today.
Innocent irredentist hearts, frustrated spirits, fragmented
consciences remembered by many in bipolar images.
Africa's post-colonial first-born tragedy,
an unlikely liberation story, neither Angola nor Azania,
sad and sour pioneer reinforcer of a continent's stigma.

News of the Desert Colonel's Death

Turn by turn
bewildered world and local leaders
take leave of their self-created quagmires,
the abode of their gloating self-congratulations
at the town-crier's notice of unusual death
In the Desert-Caesar's blood-soaked dusty dry sewer
foretelling the demise of a dreaded Empire.

Our own leaders in shock disbelief
watch the painful clips shamefacedly
the defunct Emperor's bloodied face,
torn turban, projected on massive screens
their own charmed futures as former
pliant and adoring subjects turn executioners
feeding imperial limbs to starving street hounds.

Our rulers see lineages and raging hordes
that once saluted the Emperor's box
now signal the gladiator's kill
cutting in shreds the purple robes, smashing the gold crown,
shaking the once adored tinsel throne to its core,
as crowds bay for the return of power and wealth built
on plunder and pillage of fruits of their lives and work.

The Desert Colonel's Last Ride

Blood rode the chariot with the Colonel,
blood on his face, blood on his hands,
blood on his robes, blood on his torn turban,
blood on the conscience of forty years of silence.
Blood turning poor, young, naive warriors
scapegoats in history's unfolding irony, into
blood judges, blood jurors, blood executioners.
Bloodied gold pistol, bloodied useless dollar bills
in Sirte's dusty boiling streets, its sleepy
sewer holes now crimson execution cells.
Blood rode the chariot with the Colonel
Hummers, Cadillac, Range Rovers, all
garlands of humiliation.
Blood rode the last winged chariot with the Colonel.

I Cannot Deny My God

I cannot deny my God.
Mad or not, vindictive or petty,
it is my God.
From its sacred springs,
I drink streams of poisoned waters,
inuring, blunting empathy,
drowning compassion, corroding judgment,
condemning to fiery execution
infidels and all locked in vile heresy.

I cannot deny my God.
Even when his infallible law
carry neither rhyme nor reason,
it is my God.
I wear the sword, dream of vestal virgins,
make bombs, ride the heathens' planes,
prepare my feasts of deathly orgy,
invite all around to our collective Golgotha
displayed proudly on the Internet the morning after.

I cannot deny my God.
Though I no longer know the truth,
it is my God.
I neither hear nor see his true prophets,
as my anger destroys deserts and forests,
I bear the cross, follow the star, crack
under the weight of the crescent and the om,
I remain your deranged, faithful bigot,
living this tormented hell on earth.

I cannot deny my God.
False prophets and compromised clergy or not,

it is my God.
Generations of child and women spoilers,
bald-headed men of gluttony,
bearded sowers of post-modern hatred,
swearing perverted truths on irreversible Word,
thriving in giving the young stones for bread,
locking women and children in dungeons of faith.
But I cannot deny my God.

We Just Want Them to Disappear

No, we don't want to kill them,
we just want them unseen, unheard,
disappeared from our presence.
We want all these different strange ones,
unlike us true natives, real believers,
to dissolve like frail morning mists
that cloud the mirrors and screens of our lives.

No, we don't want to silence them,
we just want them unheard, unloved,
their voices, songs and dances stilled.
We want all these so weird and queer,
unlike us regular, straight and normal,
muffled, crippled, neutered, muted and blinded,
living in blissful distant harmony in their leper's colony.

No, we don't hate or despise them,
we just want them unloved, unwanted,
their laughter, happiness and prayers stopped.
We want all these of another color and creed
Who pray, love and worship differently,
unlike us the only true children of the true God,
crucified, guillotined, amputated, buried alive
in concrete and steel tombs of our delusions and denial.

Forbidden Script, Taboo Learning

This script that alien Empire undergirds
from the Mediterranean to the Pacific,
from sandy Sahara to frozen Tundra,
bearing pacification and foreign order
is taboo, a sacrilege, forbidden, cursed.

This script prescribes laws that chain us,
re-writes our stories, records forced
taxes, affirms trade with usury, distort
days and moons with infidel cycles, steals
our tongues, silences voices, erase ceremonies,
desecrate sacred places.

This script, in language that unknown gods speak,
turns our sons slaves to Mammon,
sends our daughters shameless
to the streets and beds of strangers, corrupting
young and old, man and woman, scholars and lay-folk.

This script demeans us, defiles our shrines, shames our gods
These evil books must be burnt, their message,
cultures, lives, all they stand for erased as we claim
our true word, the one and only script, learning, and laws
of the true and only god, no other, none but our god
in our book-burning, unforgiving, other-denying righteous
fury.

Angry Souls, Arid Lands

A curious traveler,
I have journeyed far and wide.
Found all types of soils and souls,
angry hearts in steely grips, woven
around drought-stricken cassava tubers
that defy death, deny starvation in rhythms
of struggles between mean nature and meaner spirits,
yielding neither harvests nor fertile
bounties of green and comforting grace.
Abodes of dust storms, hostile, other-hating,
denying rest to the weary traveler from afar,
rejecting goodwill and prayer foretold in the stars.
Here emotions and bodies are starved,
welcome gongs muffled, joyful drums silenced,
peals of laughter blunted, smiles smothered, trees
and oases stripped, customs and rites scattered,
cooling bowls for dusty feet broken, soothing waters
for parched throats split. Only suspicion, stale and gritty
hostility, dusty, cold and piercing, AK47s and gun wagons
reign, as arid soils are bent in submission to barren cruel souls.

What Kind of Misogynist Brother?

Cocoons of abuse and prejudice
threaten in cold death embrace,
to smother in sickly perfumed crypt
of acceptably patriarchal daily mores and saws!
In harsh rude riffs, we get rap and hip hop
that oppress the mind, pepper the inner eye,
as unwashed male mouths chant and cheer,
stealing from politics to remake in diluted brews,
polluted, unpalatable, twisted to hatred
for sisters, daughters and mothers of our lives,
their choruses and songs that demean women,
deny, desecrate our sisters, making me writhe in pain
between thoughtful rigor and makeshift figuring out:
What kind of misogynist brother are you?
Explanations and rationalizations drown me
in family guilt, sibling denial, blood betrayal.
But no to comforting crypts of male excuses.
Beyond beer parlor reflexes of blood, color and sex
layers of prejudice and abuse must be stopped,
wherever they may be found.

On the Image of an African Child in a Fund-raising Advert

My heart in anguish screams at church,
schools, charities, do-good public, at your
dark media image of our sorry
kwashiorkor-stomach infants, scum on nostrils
faces tear-scarred crying from suffering's whips.
You relive in your campaigns, oppression,
diminishing our redemption songs, you lay bare
poverty's violation replaying our sensuality of suffering,
recalling for us the sad ancient Marquis
in actions that twice demean. Our sorrows, you
pimp for distant sympathy and money,
our images you use to arouse believers and haters,
you display our poor undressed, unwashed, unloved,
stripped of dignity, you seek sympathy twisted in
worthless truss of collective contempt, prejudice
and scorn that subliminal race and creed build.

Light Is Not White

Light is not always white
as shadow is not always black.
Light is bronze, silver, and gold
that love and hope beam,
many colored counters to hate and despair.

Light shines through tunnels of evil; clear
pathways amid daily cobwebs
everywhere, waves and vibes that borders
and boundaries of race and nation defy,
binding hearts again, restoring spirits, arousing hope.

Light is not always white
as ideologues and bigots make believe
in the blindness of their world of shadows.
Light is perennial contest, unending tussles,
and undying fights with unbridled greed,
malice unrestrained, deception made triumphant
by the powerful as they smother our lives
with mounds of sugary illusions and delusions
in pursuit of privileged happiness that others exclude.

It matters not what man, beast or spirit,
what art, vocation, business or craft,
or what God they proclaim or confess,
they carry darkness when they carry hate.

Tunes of Hope

I see change in cascading rhythms
of ordinary people's lives, a dance here,
a skip there, passionate flips, acrobats
that find beats to map roads to nowhere.

I see change in dried tear paths on
fading grandmother's cheeks, chants
laced with proverbs, old mama wisdom,
carrier of secrets unveiling the sorry nudity
of the prancing patriarch's frailty,
fiery terror and daily and nightly oppression,
sad noise flattened into dry flaccid waste.

Grandmothers and mothers, bless their souls,
remain backbones of our battered integrity,
smiling in daily irony at the suffering wrought
by powerless gestures of the insecure ruler's swagger stick.

I see change in smiles that dance, in sunlight
embroidered in faces, hopeful twists of defiant waists,
hisses from souls unbowed, uncowered, unyielding
to wasted Chiefs afraid of their stalking shadows,
inner beings in contempt cast out, finished spirits
awaiting the dung hill fires of the people's sacrifice.

I see change as men and women sweat out their dances,
girls and boys work out songs. I know that not
many days soon drummers of change will play
tunes of hope in the heart of the land, as our people
gather to build and reset in the light of a new dawn.

Upbeats

Moments

There's a moment of nylon flight,
thin gray line between here and there,
when imagination's lush suds lather reality,
and creativity finds its cleansing expression
in the flow of palm wine.

There's a moment in anger,
when the blocked energy,
granite boulder frustration of the mind,
finds release in emotion's canal flows,
through the Nile of our feelings
into wombs of our Lake Victoria.

There's a moment in a depressed state,
when all dark depths of tension,
holes and valleys of despair are overcome;
we forgive ourselves and others for sins
known, unknown, imagined, felt or real,
opening up torrents of unprecedented conversations.

There's a moment in love
when the light of understanding
on faith, belief and trust appear,
driven by intuition and rare knowledge,
universal forces that mark unique humanity
flowing up from the blind pits of surrender.

There's a moment of peace,
when pain and anger are remembered,
vengeance and remorse dissolve, acceptance fragrances,
purifying life's complicated routes, and scents
laced with sorrow, joy, love and hate
endlessly unfold unexpected intentions and acts.

There's a moment in life,
when we defy the normal foundations of our being,
schooling and rearing that unprepared us all,
as we find firm answers in anchors of feathers,
in seas of smiles, frowns and tears,
flows from our inner core of human frailty.

My Jordan Moment

My Jordan moment often comes
with its own little white dove
on my shoulders, in grace descending
with slight flutters, bringing light
on wings sacred and rare.
Bright light glinting,
not in recognition,
not in anointment,
but in rays of mindfulness,
my spirit overwhelmed, in torment,
surrender and unrelenting adoration.
My body, soul, and mind in humility bending,
my being filled, weighed, overflowing
with love that cleanses remorse and regrets,
amazing grace coursing through veins
of my wanderer's soul, lost and found,
now reclaimed, awakened, unbound.

Our Songs

Where did all the songs go?
Songs of joy, songs of sorrow,
songs to dance, songs to weep,
songs to live for, songs to sleep.

Where did all the songs go?
Birds humming, winds whistling,
leaves crackling, rains splattering,
children's steps drumming the earth.

Where did all the songs go?
The rhythms of the forests,
harmonies of the plains and mounts,
melodies of the waters and winds.

Where did all the songs go?
Expressions of Nature's grace,
bearers of anger and pleasure,
music of life, death and renewal.

Bonfire for the Year End

Harmattan crusty winds,
winter's ear-biting chill,
heralds of the coming of the feast
across the lands I know as home.
The season signals year end, declares festive
times, though life and movements proceed
in new-found wilder frenzy, gifts to give,
markets brimming with buyers and goods.
God help the chicken, goats and rams, their destiny
tied to stew pots, pepper soup and festive grills adorn.
In our rejoicing at another year end,
I stop to mark the moment,
light a bonfire for all my woes.
One by one last year's pains and regrets I toss.
The spites, insults, neglects and loss I discard,
the abuse, anger, hate and malice I cast off.
The foaming bitterness that cloud reason I spit out.
One by one the bonfire consumes my year's sorrows.
Each motion a tribute to memory, each gesture
releases the sighs, sweat and tears of burdens borne.
I cede the pain and disappointments to the passing year,
build anew a cauldron of thanks and graces,
for the love, compassion, mercies that endured.
For the gentle touch, warm embrace, kind smiles,
the sympathetic tone of comforting voices, the Gibraltar
presence of unquestioning love, undenied, freely given.
In this season of year end grace and mercies, I arrange
flowers here, plants there, vines to build my thanks
because knowing and loving you all dear friends and family
made my life's goodness blossom and flower.

Tuning the Word, Tuning the Drums

In the word is
the annunciation, the anointment
the beginning, the birth
the creation, the communion
the damnation, the death
the emotion, the elation
the feeling, the form
the light, the love
the moment, the meaning
the prayer, the peace
the redemption, the rising
the story, the song
the silence, the solace
the test, the torment
the yearning, the yielding
the zenith and zero.

I find the word, feel the word,
hold the word, hug the word,
kiss the word, keep the word,
love the word, live the word,
make the word, mar the word,
pray the word, preach the word,
reject the word, redeem the word,
say the word, sing the word,
taste the word, tune the word,
test the word, try the word,
view the word, voice the word,
wear the word, weave the word.

In the word
I find all beings, all things, and nothingness.

Stirrings at Dawn

Dew droplets at dawn,
glitter of tiny diamonds
on soul's receptive petals.
Light hesitant kisses,
gentle feathery nibbles
on morning's ear lobes.
Voyeur birds their joy chirp
as insistent Sun rays spear
sweet love through clouds
from a proud rising Day
that lover Earth embrace.
The morning stirs and stretches,
clasped in wakefulness mists
adrift from Night's sleep comfort.

The Wakefulness of a Long Night

As sleep's sweet scented blanket eludes me,
blue, green, red lights twinkle in the dark,
I watch the night with neighborhood hounds,
deranged patrols squealing in mating, screeching in duels,
loud barks at every intruding sound and scent.
How long is the night?

As calmly I glide through the long hours
serenaded by the Four-O'Clock Mombasa train,
wheels drumming its way with protesting wagons,
fatigued from their load as they crawl past Nairobi West
tunneling the Bunyala Underpass in salute to the abandoned
Colonial Cemetery.
How long is the night?

In the paused long night,
muffled conversations of couples
mix with muted sounds of passion
seeping through cracks in windows and doors,
defying traps of unceasing lock-down lives.
How long is the night?

As morning descends in the Muezzin's recorded call
blaring from the mosque's invisible tower down South,
hastening drowsy faithfuls to cold ablution,
I hear the Ave Marias chiming from Don Bosco Marian Shrine,
beckoning another community of faithfuls to their morning
rituals.
How long is the night?

As early birdsongs greet the rising sun
searing through the clouds,

the crazy crows chorus their raucous din in search of food,
I wonder what fasts birds break at morn.
I realize that oceans from West to East were only just crossed,
Fueling jet lag and hunger that compel wakefulness bravely
borne.

Tunes from Silent Depths

Soft footsteps hushed
on lawns of padded soul,
to the Nameless one I speak.
She, we all call our own name,
so that we can truly connect
in ways and manner our own,
in moods, stories and tongues ours.

In loving tender reverence,
in inner ears of my spirit,
I hear the voice of the Beloved,
in trembling awe and admiration,
tender the love, awesome the wonder,
that tie us to deep and far longings
in immortality and redemption promise.

From trees to winds that leaves
caress, bringing relief from desert heat,
gifts from mean mountains, clean springs,
hot and cold plains and deeps,
celestial songs and chants I hear,
hot tunes and vibes that spew embers
from silent depths of everlasting heights.

Epiphany

Poetry,
is that what it is?
Secrets many layered finally unfolded,
Harmattan-season duvet of leather, felt and velvet.

Poetry,
enthralling chants of creation,
endless depths in primordial wombs,
a thousand veils of mystery and light.

Spirits,
multiple deities, ancestors of many tongues,
glittering halos of saints and martyrs,
altars to all: demons, holy and fallen angels.

Imagination,
day-time dreams of Sango
in leopard and ostrich hides dancing
with seven vestal virgins on a diamond stud.

Life,
Djinns, elves and ghosts in hats of fireflies,
beings above, here and below all in one,
one in all with ageless Mother Nature.

Intuition,
unstoppable waves, winds and wastes,
wombs and wilds, deserts and heights,
all consecrated chalices for inner knowing.

Beauty,
multi-toned and multi-scented,

beyond beholder's senses,
Joseph's coat, Southern escape route tapestry.

Hatred,
clever cruelty, blind denial,
willful ignorance insistently replayed,
as Auschwitz, Bosnia and Darfur are remade.

Poetry
fertile valley flooded
with tales of the Emperor's nudity.
Nature's blended truths, fantasies and myths,
carved as the sculptor dreams, feels, sees.

Garden of Verses

Stories are all I have to give,
baskets of tales and fables
of different scents and hue,
sizes and flavors, strung, arranged,
painstaking collections across times,
places and people to stir, arouse, bore,
anger and depress, all emotions tickle.

Stories that last, tales that wither,
fables that take many forms with
passing time.
Smooth tongue, spinner
of yarns old and new, many scents
that lift tired spirits, inspire weary
minds, lighten sorrows, offer caution
for exuberance broken loose.

Stories are the composition of life's
many level garden of mysteries where
leaves, flowers, and thorns,
you find together with worms, beetles,
butterflies, visiting sparrows, canaries,
intruder feral cats and bats, snakes
hidden deep beneath grass carpets, crickets
visiting at night with songs competing
with the bull frog's mating calls from pools,
streams, swamps, moist havens, miniature falls.

Stories from family memory dredged, clan songs
retrieved, folklore from layers of debris dug,
prizes from our lyrical archaeology. Elders' tales,
proverbs and parables offered in return for devotion,

attention, time, money and respect.
Stories are the seeds, pollen and spores that our garden
of verses and mysteries fill, my gift and yours.

Dance and Trance

Dervish spirit,
down this far South,
in colorful trance I swirl,
Sango's androgyny, skirts and braids,
singer of songs, Jeremiah's heirs.
To Anna Swir's bare bone verse I swoon,
transcendental lyrics mind and body charmed,
luminous songs, everlasting vibes that enchant.
Choruses drummed from paddles that drill Okara's rivers,
beats that string Gibran's desert to Rumi's Orient,
Okigbo's sacred forest shrines to Blake's spirits.
Songs that dissolve icy fear, unlock gilded cages
and release all from comfortable dungeons.
Shining Light on leaders who cast dark shadows,
verses that duel modern political shamans,
shame and dare spinners of our economic clouds and storms.

Poetry's Burden

Only poetry can save us,
words, songs, rhythm and rhyme
a gift to all our generations,
races, color and creed.

Only poetry can save us,
verses, chants, choir, duet and solo,
the rapper's heave, the hip hop feel, reggae chants,
concert pianist taps, street kid's barrel scratch,
emotions, motions, moments and meter
recounting our post-modern specter of lost souls,
dead spirits in digital graves awaiting resurrection morning
in cyber spaces with no place for isolated lonely souls,
endless noise in repressed ear-plug deafness,
contacts with inner selves blocked by our plug-ins.

I am sure only poetry can save us
beats, color, dance, voice, drama and sculpture,
drums, Kora, guitar, sitar, piano and horns,
strokes on canvas, strikes on wood, leather and bronze,
stones carved that speak visions new and daring,
sights, sighs, songs, strumming of hopes recovered,
joys reclaimed, sorrows tamed, pain soothed,
nerves calmed, healing in singing and dancing,
irrepressible incessant struggle to be human again.

Silk Screen of My Dreams

Now the multi-color silk screen
of my dreams I slowly see
as endless passing seasons fade
into gold and bronze dry corn fields.

My fears at every violent storm
with time and place recede,
as the mid-noon brown shores
of accepted lesser victories I face.

Though blood continue to boil,
with every charge and toil,
now I remain more content
the battles from the sideline to plot.

Daily, beads of youthful ambition
I tell, as across different altars
I offer fervent prayers
for renewal of imagination.

Fully well I know that age
may color dreams of youth,
but its winds the sturdy sails
that drive creation never breaks.

Poetry by Hand

I still write poetry by hand,
long drawn-out seduction
between pen and paper,
sensuous scribbles, day and night.
Shy first encounters, enduring impressions.
Tentative contacts, love beyond first sight.
Entranced murmurs, endlessly revised introductions,
whispered to the subject of my preoccupation.

I still hum verses in my head,
tunes irresistible, often uninvited,
melodious intruders of my wandering being.
Insistent choruses from childhood playfields.
Color and image from past dreams,
drumbeats of dance in yet unforeseen futures.
Sweet, bitter, joyful, angry riffs
erupting from depths beyond reach.

I still chant rhymes aloud,
mantras from undying ancestry.
Lyrics and beats stringing together –
Sahel Sufi, Wolof Griot, Bata Dancer,
Ghetto Rapper, Happy hour rhymer, Village Crier,
all in one musical umbilical cord.
Believers in dance, sound and song,
spinners of blues, magical heat and light,
praises, prayers and curses from on high,
primordial spells to whose enchanting calls,
I do not always cry Amen.

Resolution

I celebrate the songs of the stars,
dance to the rhythms of the moon,
run with the mountain springs,
dive with the roaring falls,
open with the morn's flowers.
The cracking of the rubber tree,
are drums for my feet to skip,
the buzz of the bees, a new day song,
gifting the honey that comes with the sting
as I roll in the glitter of sunflower fields.
Life's songs await no procrastination,
their never ceasing rhythms are forever present,
each second humming a new verse,
inscribing a virgin emotion,
commanding our duty to Nature,
demanding life's daily undiluted attention.

Integrity

Dry rock island in roiling murky waters,
a safe haven taken for granted,
solid refuge, fishermen and farmer's retreat,
when daily life is flooded with deceit
and betrayal drowns all trust and belief.
The polished beam in our knowing eyes
painfully hammered deep into our very selves.
Cells and skins torn, veins shattered,
shedding torrents of disillusioned blood,
as our modern self-proclaimed prophets
abandon our principled and eternal truths
to prostrate and adore voluptuous idols.

Purification

The plastic of being
all dissolved,
the corrugated rust of living
all molten,
the tinsel of the ego
all broken.

Free and fluid was
the reality of being, effortless
the motion of selves liberating
the intensity of souls,
feeling, touching, knowing,
the flows from Nature's source
unpolluted, uninterrupted, undistorted.

Hope

We cut and paste hope
not as waste shredded,
but as History boldly reclaimed,
inscribed in living Ashanti gold blocks,
flames of many tongues
in descent at our very own Pentecost.

A Kind of Acknowledgment

Prodded and pushed,
tickled and teased,
taunted and haunted,
friends and family,
editors, poets and conscience
that will not let go.

Beats and songs you all coax
from behind hesitant lips,
long abandoned drums-ensemble,
releasing the reluctant griot and
itinerant drummer, once sealed in a silver bottle.

You help find voice
for decades tied,
spun in concepts and theories,
frameworks stuck in mundane toil.

Praise for The Wanderer's Wave

"Tade Aina's book, *The Wanderer's Waves,* is an outstanding poetic chronicle of a trailblazer's explorations, observations and experiences across the world, from the Americas to Zimbabwe and from the early years of youth. The composition style is a combination of traditional, renaissance and modernist archetypes in postcolonial poetic rendition. The poems, in total, also have a universal community spirit and reflectively speak to our blessed multiple identities as humans, while shedding clear light on the ties that bind humanity, such as ties to nature and mobility.

The poetic journey begins with attribution (of destination inspiration, knowledge and quest) to the courageous sounds and souls of two iconic poets, David Diop and Christopher Okigbo, whose tragic deaths speak to the book's curative assemblage of memories of joys and sorrows, blooms and glooms, courage and faint-heartedness, hopes and fears, and more across the world (including his beloved homeland, Nigeria). The poems also have super-creative metaphors, insightful imagery, refreshing figurative language, and diverse metering that will resonate very deeply with readers across generations in different global contexts."

– Akwasi Aidoo, author of *Rhythms of Dignity* (Amalion 2020).

"Rich-veined, sensual, and probing, this rewarding collection bears the imprint of a keen, world-wise poet. Tade Aina is a well-traveled man who weaves the lore, legends and histories of hearth and far-flung places with equal self-assurance."

– Okey Ndibe, author of *Foreign Gods, Inc.* (Soho Press 2014).

"Travel, landscapes, people, the territories of the senses, of the heart. 'Life, for him a geography of minutes'. Echoes from the experiences of the restless soul about the world, whose work also turns him into an eavesdropper, the fly-on-the-wall insights. In this body of work, to be gently savored, the reader will encounter the dimensions of worlds, refracted in a most refreshing way."

– Yvonne Adhiambo Owuor, author of *Dust* (Granta 2015).